Signs of Subversive Innocents

# Signs of Subversive Innocents

Cora Siré

George Payerle, Editor

Cover design by Doowah Design.
Cover illustration by Bruce Roberts.
Photo of Cora Siré by Otokar Pogacnik.

This book was printed on Ancient Forest Friendly paper.
Printed and bound in Canada by Hignell Book Printing Inc.

We acknowledge the support of The Canada Council for the Arts and the Manitoba Arts Council for our publishing program.

Library and Archives Canada Cataloguing in Publication

Siré, Cora
Signs of subversive innocents / Cora Siré.

Poems.
ISBN 978-1-927426-38-8

I. Title.

PS8575.P465A92 2014 C811'.6 C2014-901325-5

Signature Editions
P.O. Box 206, RPO Corydon, Winnipeg, Manitoba, R3M 3S7
www.signature-editions.com

*For the one who plays the clarinet and quena*

## Contents

### Quarry Manifesto


Quarry I 11
"Absolutely No Rubbish" 12
Magnolia Tree Project 13
The Gardener 15
Before Leaving Hué 16
Aquarians 18
Leaping into the Sea of Dreams 19
Squeeze My Heart 20
Zeitgeist 21
The Swamp in San Lorenzo 22
Manifesto of a Murdered Poet 24
Thundersnow 26


### No Loitering / Pas de flânage


Quarry II 29
On the *Tree of Life* 30
Response 31
Invitation to Travel 32
The Quena Testifies 33
Brazen Metropolis 34
History of a Muse 36
In Exile 38
Montpelier, Vermont 39
Emperor's Lake 40
Crimson Tide 41


### A Strange Pain


Quarry III 45
Predeceased 46
Vinci da Leonardo to Homage 47
Snarl 48
Her Human Voice 49

Amor y Muerte 50
A Dios 52
Rendition *n.* (often followed by *of*) 53
Three Canvas Train Ride 54
Dance 57
A Pacific Vision 58

## Pale Blue Light

Quarry IV 63
Cordillera Midnight 64
The Last Grenade 65
Polar Spheres 66
Nightfall in Sai Gon 67
Dac Drums the Drums 70
Warrior 71
Itinerant & Stalker 72
Buried Alive 74
Miscarriage 75
Small Reveals 76
Miraculous Montage of the Morning Mind 77
Reprise 79

End Notes 81
Acknowledgements 82
About the Author 83

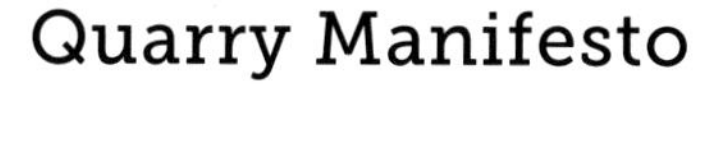

## Quarry I

We've often passed this masterpiece
carved with ice-age grace
into the roadside woods.
This time he indulges me.
We leave the car, walk single file
towards the water's edge.
I strain to discern our reflections
on a looking glass flecked
by shedding birch trees,
October leaves floating in clusters
within the marble's craggy ledges.

While so intensely visual,
the first effect is audible
as screams and laughter
echo from a season ago
when beach towels draped the boulders
and swimmers cooled off until dusk.
Some kissed, shared a joint
and shivered at the glimpse of starbursts
atop the surface of the pond, tiny halos
of refracted light on the rippling blackness.

And later, in the moonlight,
they fumbled with buttons and zippers
then scrambled up a ledge
to mark the marble
*Evan ♥ Hannah 1997*
more pledge than defacement,
the way a scar makes
beauty interesting,
that has me ponder, is this
the place to chisel your love?

## "Absolutely No Rubbish"

Nothing trashy about this admonition
someone carved into stained wood
before painting each letter a cheerful yellow.
Authoritative
a comfort in tough times
a literary rule of thumb or
the motto of a cell of ecoterrorists.
It's classy too, egg yolk on hazelnut,
although one could argue
the adverb's redundant.
The sign, compact and thus poetic,
allows no space to claim a middle ground.
So why do I feel like sticking my gum
into the O of the NO?

## Magnolia Tree Project

White tufts spring out among our coils of limbs
a creamy bliss bouqueted in tangled sheets.
Then summer's angst prevails and passion dims
white tufts wither among the coils of limbs
and icy blankets sterilize our sins
until the solar power of our bond defeats
all brittleness and from a coil of limbs
a creamy bliss springs forth from tangled sheets.

*You wrote this...*his voice trails off
but she hears *piece of crap*, thinks
nap sap lap flap rap map zap
and in defence explains the feat
of finding an appropriate rhyme for sheet.
*My passion never dims!* he says
and then more kindly adds,
*but creamy bliss is good.*
He puts the piece of paper down
the verse read once
born of a battle with wretched angst.

Two twisted trunks fatally connected
exposed to winter's wind, ice, sleet and snow
until the thaw gently resurrected
two twisted trunks. Fatally connected
they unfurl leafy shoots on branches flecked
with buds that blossom to a pink-white show.
Two twisted trunks fatally connected
expose spring's passion with a flowery snow.

*The second triolet is truer to its form,*
a poet friend weighs in,
*but it's so fatalistic and*
*I want to know more about the lovers.*
*Pass the cashews please?*

Who dares in this sardonic age of terror
to write of love as a magnolia tree?
May shrapnel rain pain and shame on the poet
who dares. In this sardonic age of terror
can the carnal be compared to pure
blossoms of tender, fleeting beauty?
Who cares? In this sardonic age of terror
why write of love? For a magnolia tree?

## The Gardener

Someone tells of beauty
in springtime furrows scraped
by the uneven quills of his rake.

He works bent over and intent
until the sun leaves an intimate
aura of red over distant hills.

Before trudging home
a cherry tree demands
his eye for form and design

so he grasps the bark
to shake confetti blossoms
over the columns of characters

in his raked calligraphy
that tells of how nothing lasts
and celebrates asymmetry.

Then he leaves for soup
entrusting his wabi-sabi
garden to the moon song

and in his absence, the flawed
beauty of scattered petals
wilt in celebration.

## Before Leaving Hué

On the Thien Mu Pagoda sacred grounds
a young monk sits in the frangipani shade
where songbirds harmonize the afternoon's
intense humidity. And stirring from
his meditative trance, he addresses me,
his voice a gong's lingering vibration
his English soft yet penetrating,
"You must visit Thúy before you leave Hué."

I'm walking to the relic on display
a rusting blue car driven by the monk
who set himself on fire in '63.
Tomorrow's my last day in this city
devoted to its poets, their verses
woven into conical hats that shield
the scars of mines and agent orange.
I follow the bleached path back to the piers
to board a blue and yellow dragon boat
as sunset streaks the Perfume River sky.
The boatman steers through swirling currents
then cuts the motor to save gas. We float
with purpose, direction, but in no rush.
He docks, I rise to disembark and pay.
Ten thousand sorrows map the boatman's eyes.
"Please visit Thúy," he says, "before leaving Hué."

I savour my last night's meal in Hué
seated on wicker by riverside lights,
not a pinch of the vague in the chillies,
turmeric, fish sauce, roasted cashews
balanced by sweet, potent *café glacé*.
An ancient woman, frail yet dignified
in her white silk *ao dai*, slips me Thúy's card
with a whisper, "*Il faut la visiter.*"

Under the hammer of Hué's morning sun
my *xich lo* driver pedals the labyrinth
of streets and alleys, past shaded shops
where raw silks hang inert, dazed by the heat.
We swerve and skid on tracks of pebbled ruts
and I gesture, "Let me walk the rest" but
he cycles on, eyes glazed, body bent by
psychic will that I visit Thúy today.

I find her inside a one-room shelter
seated in a dome of lemony sun
shafting sideways through a paneless window.
In a slow-motioned circle around her
women prepare palm leaves, cut threads and twill,
smooth back loosened strands of her fine black hair.
I'm seated on a stool in the corner
as if awaited by Thúy on my last day
as if she understands that all of Hué
has sent me here to witness the making
of a poem, a sacred act in this land
where suffering spans centuries of stanzas.
She bows over the work between her feet,
images and words cut from black paper.
Among layers of translucent palm leaves
Thúy weaves her cosmos, weightless yet concrete.

Hours of sweat before she's satisfied
and the poem is offered into sunlight
revealing silhouettes of lovers lost,
songbirds and a riverside pagoda,
six lines of verse in Vietnamese.
She points with her one handless arm
at the embedded name I won't forget,
Thúy, the poet I met before leaving Hué.

## Aquarians

we chain-smoked Camel cigarettes
we got beach tar on our feet
we put a candle in the window
we believed there'd be an answer

we looked at the ivy on the old clinging wall
we learned where the grapes of wrath are stored
we requested amor por favor
we were so good with words

we watched your every breath
we planted love and let it grow
we rocked you gently with our song
we cried for Argentina

we got a shirt that we really loved
we bought, oh Lord, a Mercedes Benz
we found a place to stay and a place to go
we got stuck in traffic, not moving anywhere

we booked a one-way ticket to paradise
we watched you standing by the ocean's roar
we hated that sadness in your eyes
we felt nothing but a heartache

we were very superstitious
we went down to the river to pray
we tried to find a reason to believe
we saw fire and we saw rain

we remembered when rock was young
we tried to relax and take it easy
we squandered our resistance
we saw the damage done

we didn't draw the queen of hearts
we didn't all call the tune
we didn't really give peace a chance
we didn't celebrate the blaze of light in every word

## Leaping into the Sea of Dreams

She rises to the angel's
kiss in a room detached
from earthliness and
empties luggage on the ceiling
to smell the floating continents,
her mother's coffee traded
for her father's violin.
Then she leaps through her window
to plunge into the city sky
and tastes the bluest oxygen,
hears yellow dance
sees orange cry.
In the noisy heights
of her deep-sea worlds
she captures fragrant lotus
and swims her story true.
Endorphins foster focus
as she soars toward the seabed
resisting weights of gravitas.
She swirls up controversial sands
and treads across
the stars.

## Squeeze My Heart

Spare me
the solitary hemlock
and arrhythmic heirloom clock,
the lace of briny foam on sable shores,
your frostbite during morning chores
and those syrup-slathered pancakes
in the diners of your criss-crossed tours.

Spare me
the hunkering harvester
and wisecracking weed whacker,
the tongue-dangling sheepdog
and your tuqued-up pal,
the puck hog.

Spare me
your getting-here traffic woes,
the sleazy slouch of your pose,
throat-clearing horks
and your monochrome delivery skills.

Poet
I'm desperate to hear
your thrills, taste your loves
and smell beauty you hold close,
touch your epiphanies and
desperations, your hatreds,
the grotesque and gross.
Play the part
and give me chills,
let me feel your hand
squeeze my heart,
get me dancing to your words.
Insult me, noble poet, I'm not afraid
of ingenuity or insanity
but I'm terrified of drowning
among snapshots of banality.

## Zeitgeist

So it's a dreary December, the sun a low ember
behind ashen snowfall, when you see him bicycle by.
You know this guy! His paintbrush, you've seen it fly
as watery blues and greys create a feisty pigeon
perched atop a tarnished angel's head.
His pedals rotate in slow-mo, one hand steadies
the handlebar and with the other, the artist grasps his heavy
canvas as he churns onward through the sooty snow.
You've seen him talking miles per minute while red paint
slashed out the cavorting grace of two horses, saddleless and free
in a generous space, leaving you (that's his gift) to imagine
context, landscapes.
He's put in *his* feistful years in your callous neighbourhood
and laughs through the fickle flash of art-collecting
nouveau riche, anchored by love (you think) and devotion to
unbridled metaphors.
So it's more than reassuring to witness his zany progress,
a distant haloed fleck cycling through the snowy solstice
delivering art despite the twilight's
falling ashes.

## The Swamp in San Lorenzo

Four sisters
and their school friends
splayed in deck chairs
by a pool of turquoise in decay
swap stories *did he really?*
and conspire *I swear he did,*
by the sunken reservoir
inlaid with azure tiles
chipped and fading now.

The girls perspire, get high on fumes
of purple lime-green coral rose,
painting their toes outside the villa
built by a stepfather's great grandmother,
first cousin to General Perón.
They never pause to think of him,
to notice shadows cast by *tipa* trees
across neglected grass
still spongy from the Christmas rains.

In the nearby city
they play piano, sing in choirs
memorize the epic poetry *aquí me pongo a cantar*
of the gaucho *como la ave solitaria*
who consoles himself with song
like the solitary songbird.
This month of holidays
spent swampside in the hills of San Lorenzo
they turn a deeper shade
amber to mahogany
except the youngest with red hair
who pouts because her freckles only multiply.

Near dusk
four sisters and their school friends
plunge into the choler of turquoise decadence
float                    limbs splayed.
Their rippling strands of hair
entrap cicada corpses
while in the deep
a rusty drain is clogged by
*tipa* flowers,
the laurels of a decomposing ovenbird
called *hornero* here
a tiny pit left by its missing eyeball.

## Manifesto of a Murdered Poet

*In your chamber covered with reverie, make waste*
*Of flowers and of spiritual lights; my soul,*
*Shod in silence and dressed in calm,*
*Will go after you down the darkest path of this night.*

Delmira Agustini, "The Encounter"
translated by Alejandro Cáceres

Poets, sisters of the spoken word
Craft your postings well
Embrace all vagary, take courage
As daily you sit down to write
Dig deep and then dig deeper.
Stare down the blackest stain
Neither slam your laptop nor abandon words
Repeat, repeat until you are depleted
Then begin anew to wrestle time and space.
*In your chamber covered with reverie, make waste*

Of pressure and rejection,
Advice and coping tips.
Waltz naked with your demons
Make music to your nervous tics.
Prepare to be misunderstood and marginalized
Condemned, lamented — eulogized.
Take on your time with all its complications
Unearth the essence and subvert
Adornments, lyrics full
*Of flowers and of spiritual lights; my soul*

Will guide you into galaxies
Past intrigue, critics and the con-men.
Expect no solace from the stars.
Once in my anguished loneliness
I confessed insanity to Rubén Darío.
His response? "To live, to live
Is the obligation of happiness."
Nonsense! Wear your isolation like a badge
Bask in the halo of melancholy, your body strong
*Shod in silence and dressed in calm.*

Torment your soul with authenticities
Be clever with your prophecies
Inoculate yourself from fear
Love in multiples and deeply.
But take care with how you die:
Leave no trace for misinterpretation
Shred all drafts, deletions, doodles
As every ink stain you've created,
Digitized or reproduced in black and white
*Will go after you down the darkest path of this night.*

## Thundersnow

He could be a retiree
in Ste. Anne de Beaupré
his only son in Afghanistan.

He rakes his property all day
then stands back at dusk
to survey the result

already missing
the leafy red/yellow broadloom
that once crackled underfoot.

Snow begins to clot in pointillist
flecks over the desolation of his
half-acre plot.

Inside, no emails or messages
from CFB Val Cartier
but later in his bed

he hears the distant bagpipe
thrum of thundersnow
and knows the worst is yet to come.

# No Loitering / Pas de flânage

## Quarry II

The percussion of hammers
and chisels resounds
as I lapse back
see shirtless men shape
hearths and headstones
commissioned by New England's
early settlers.
Massive slabs are heaved
onto flatbed wagons
while oxen stamp impatiently
in the morning mist.

The train whistles off
delivering the marble
to scaffoldings raised for Yankee
mansions, churches, banks
and new world industry.
Then a death knell
in the hands of artists
sculpting monuments and tombs
to enshrine Civil War corpses.

Abruptly
not a sound.
The quarry abandoned in 1915,
stacks of blasted boulders
like stale, greying marshmallows
stranded along walls of unmined marble.
Vertical scars
leave just enough space for
            birch trees
to sprout
            in between.
A plaque adorns this place of immortality
*Dorset Quarry established 1785*
a headstone less the date of death,
a cemetery unto itself.

## On the *Tree of Life*

The humble sculpture,
metal and postcard-sized, hangs
from my bedroom wall:
tiny humans clamber up
outstretched branches of the tree.
Just your initial
etched beside the year *80*
in the corner, so
35 years from the date
your twin sisters hanged themselves.
What was your intent?
Vision of how things might have
been or living tomb?
You, whose mother helped you flee
from advancing Russian troops,
lived your sculptor's fate
while the twins were left behind.
*Ride west!* they'd been told
but they rigged ropes from rafters
in fear of capture and rape.
Are they among those
figures in your tree? Hammered
out in angry strokes
wrestling with survivor guilt
in your Paris atelier.
Or are the humans
us, your living relatives?
Yes, that could be me
among the figures scrambling
heavenward inside the tree
straining with a load
of genetic memory,
doomed by DNA
imprisoned in your metal
perpetual refugees.

# Response

*Dear friend... With reference to your desire to share my daily life,*
*I may say that you will be staying with me if I am out of prison...*
Gandhi to Bonhoeffer in a 1935 letter

Dawn. He climbs the scaffolding and prays
unheard words in the fog of Flossenbürg.

Afterwards decades crackle and hiss.
Self-indulgence, cheap rhymes
strewn across the century's wasted graves
*the self-observed observing Mind*
in quatrains of cliché and *utterly banal.*
Where was the homage to courage, Wystan?

Pastor, prison writer, poet
raised his voice for the voiceless
chose Tegel when he could have gone to India.
(Imagine a meeting of *Satyagraha* and *Widerstand*
G: My friend, we suffer and do not submit to the laws.
B: *Ja*, death is the supreme festival on the road to freedom.)
For his resistance, Friday's child was hanged at thirty-nine.

Decades smoulder on. The promise of
*some total gain or loss* is proven hollow.
Gurus laugh disarmingly
claim survival begs for meditation.
Mantras fly with space debris
through a chorus of persistent words.
Cynics pause, what about poetic arrogance
repudiation? When there's no time for cheap grace
reload memory draw mercy and resist.

Wisps of steam rise from his corpse
another body tossed on a pile. Flames.

## Invitation to Travel

At Tim Horton's off the 417 in a franco-Ontario town,
the *flâneurs* gather to bypass chagrin,
nurse coffees and finger car keys
the idle way they used to flick their cigarettes.

They trade anecdotes
for gossip, prices for the scores,
eyes fixed on outsiders
revolving in and out the doors.

Mistrust protects a hard-fought land
yet their gaze betrays a yearning
as if these *flâneurs* await an invitation
from a stranger they would call *itinérant.*

Beneath the red sign cloned in many elsewheres
they sit enclosed like the rarest flowers
by windows streaming summer/winter sun,
their uniqueness never celebrated in any *hymne à la beauté.*

Oh subversive innocents!
A few metres outside on the concrete wall
the sign warns:
No Loitering / *Pas de flânage.*

They're likely unaware of Baudelaire
and dare not dream of travel this late in life
but if a vagabond would summon them
*Mon enfant, ma soeur*

each one of these *flâneurs*
would stand submissively,
step through the doors and
follow to the poet's distant land.

## The Quena Testifies

the cadence of the Urubamba
the yellow trills of siskin birds
the howl of winds that sweep the peaks
the thunder of the sliding rocks
the gliding beat of condor wings
the llamas skittering across the ridge
the threshers in the coca fields
the drench of rain that ricochets
the dance of maize in terraces
the carnivals of tumbling joy
the purple sway of orchids
the fragile fluttering of ferns
the gasp of air so thin
the knowing glint of sunrise
the thirst of weaponry
the blood-red clay of cliffs
the rumble of the quaking earth
the curse of occupation
the echoes of the fallen stars
the indifference of the heavens
the drumbeats of a massacre
the ruins of the civilized
the vertigo of homelessness
the flickering eyes of disappeared
the urgent cries of *nunca más*
to all this the *quena* testifies

## Brazen Metropolis

It thrills me still
the night-long flight
down the Andean spine
until hues of dawn ignite
the thread of Amazon
and the plane descends
into the swarm of sleepless streets,
*palacios* with balconied facades
corroded by the blood of history,
*palo borrachos* and jacarandas
competing in a skyward race with
glitzy global tombs.

I flow along the melodies
Corrientes, Suipacha, Libertador
and in the chaos of the city streets
discern the poets' legacies:
Borges' promise of adventure,
Storni's lines to the sadness of Buenos Aires
and Lowell who flew home in a straitjacket
"a thousand miles from nowhere."

My first time here in 1983
the city stirred from the six year
Dirty War like a necropolis
resurrected from its marble chill.
By Recoleta's vaults and mausoleums
the kneeling congregations sang
Oh save us inside Pilar Church.
The walls of ochre, white
built by their hands
responded with the silence of denial.

When, forgive me, I was naive and bold,
I asked about the outlines of bodies
spray-painted on sidewalks in the night
and the women with white headscarves

who circled the Plaza de Mayo
Thursday afternoons, I was told
*de eso no se habla*
30,000 disappeared
of this one does not speak.

The junta's scars still fester,
the infection's never treated,
a congenital malignancy in the
sniffed-out eyes of a kid on Libertador.
If his hands cannot deliver
enough *carpincho* wallets to the strong man on the block,
this *pibe* will sleep hungry on his cardboard square
beneath the portal to Chacarita Cemetery,
Borges' "slum for souls."

And yet the miracle of murals in the alleys,
poetry in plazas, the *bandoneón* in bars,
milongas reinvented, amplified,
the edgy wonder, the flash, the jokes
the time to linger and debate
the city's recent bauble,
a sixty-six-foot flower of steel
with solar-powered petals that close at dusk
an evening reverence, folding into itself in prayer.

Nights are brash in Buenos Aires
with the glint and glitter
of the sprawling grid
laid out like sabres, swords and daggers.
Amid the defiant razzle dazzle,
popping corks, the swish of silk,
I hear despair
in the rattling wheels of makeshift carts
as *cartoneros* in the thousands
scavenge through the trash.

## History of a Muse

Take a look at her now while she's asleep,
the mermaid physique, long, lithe and steep,
stretching across the cordillera
to the tierra del fuego at her feet.

When she was young, she welcomed the ships
on the docks of her port with a sway to her hips.
Immigrants came from Italy and Spain
finding safety and shelter after dangerous trips.

These craftsmen constructed her monuments,
spacious avenues, gardens and convents.
They built her an opulent opera house
with velvet loges and gilt ornaments.

Her neighbourhood danced to strumming guitars,
men duelled tangos outside crowded bars,
poets wrote lyrics extolling her grace
while she swivelled and dipped under stars.

Soon she dressed in haute couture and black tights
topped by silver fox stoles on winter nights.
With her stiletto heels and sultry gait,
her elegance rose to superlative heights.

She craved power and uniformed men,
seducing the ranks until her flirtations
flourished to generals. The cruellest hooked her
on the drug called domination.

She became known for her extravagance
secretly stowing gold bars in Swiss banks.
She financed hospitals and schools
and with the change, bought aircraft, guns and tanks.

But she couldn't handle criticism,
left-wing agitation, communism.
Her neuroses soon degenerated
into paranoia. With her trusty weapon,

an obedient armed forces,
she ordered clandestine sources
to incarcerate perceived enemies.
Prisons filled, so live torsos

dropped from death flights into seas
or were lined along trenches on their knees
for mass executions in open fields.
Her vengeance became a vicious disease.

While overspending on jewels and fur,
she coveted islands and declared war.
Former friends and neighbours, sick
of her arrogance, ganged up on her.

The new boyfriend loved globalization
more than he loved his declining nation,
she who let him rape and rob her blind
with peso conversions, privatization.

Too late for her they legalized divorce.
Now, depleted and beyond remorse,
she sleeps all day then rifles in dumpsters
and rants about her islands taken by force.

## In Exile

You remember a pillowcase,
was it peach, eggshell or yellow?
You know it smelled of marzipan,
the world-worn linen embroidered
with an unfamiliar monogram.
White cross-stitching healed its rips,
a gentle friction on your fragile skin.
Marta, her name was, scrubbed
the bedding weekly with an ochre bar,
let you blow off bubbles from the basin.
She hung your pillowcase from a cord
strung between two coral trees.
It dried in minutes under that searing sun.
Nights it overheard your dreams
whispered incantations
and your screams through dangerous
journeys yet to come.
Someone's shoeshine rag by now
but was it peach, eggshell or yellow?

# Montpelier, Vermont

A cold drive south
we have of it, me and Otokar,
even jeeps take it slow on the I-89
as snow smothers the last bales
and sumac drowns by the mile
their bloody tips craning out of drifts
to the convulsions of windshield wipers
our only weaponry against the insurgent white.
We swerve down the exit ramp
slither past clusters of the intrepid
on their lunch hours. The country's highest
concentration of pacifists
convene for soup and dialogue
undeterred by the invasive storm.
Our wheels skid at the first red light
the Jetta angling into the shoulder
in front of a living tree. At first giddy relief
we missed the bundled pedestrians
crossing Main Street but then we see the sign
nailed to the bark of the tree:
Hunters
No Rifles Buckshot Only
*What's buckshot?* I ask Otokar.
*It's the ammo used in shotgun shells.*
And I had thought they were different here.

## Emperor's Lake

I cross a footbridge in Hué today,
and it sways with every step, to a pavilion
where concubines once lounged
          while Emperor Tu Duc wrote poetry.
I should be calmed by songbirds in the frangipani trees
but it's 1883, Tu Duc is dying.
French cannons rumble to the lake and
clicking bayonets silence the cicadas.
Concubines lay lotus flowers on his tomb in the pagoda
while Tu Duc sits down to write his final poem.

I cross a footbridge at nine in the morning
and it quivers in the haze of heat
above the water's surface
          inlaid with lotus flowers.
I should be lulled by crimson blossoms
but it's 1968, Tu Duc's heirs are celebrating Tet
unaware of VC warriors creeping from the tunnels.
Fireworks disguise exploding weapons
aimed at soldiers smoking Marlboros by the lake
until the bullets hit.

I falter on the undulating footbridge
down the hill from the pagoda
          mirrored in miniature
on the Emperor's lake.
I should be pacified by squadrons of goldfish
but it's 2004, twenty-nine years since war
sank mines beneath the lotus flowers and
the offspring of the soldiers once stationed by this lake
are deployed in Iraq, their destiny foreshadowed here.

I cross history in Hué today
          and it sways with every step.
I seek refuge in the shade of the pavilion
then retreat towards the future,
same bloody path as the past.

## Crimson Tide

The convoys rumble into Mandalay
soldiers assemble by our compound's gate
I hear the crush of boots and pray
to Buddha then rise to face my fate.

At dawn the crowd assembles by our gate
and we walk barefoot from the pagoda
to join the brave resisting Burma's fate
as rifles aim, fire shots and are reloaded.

My brothers' blood pools by the pagoda
clouds of tear gas thicken over the gate
more shots are fired, rifles cranked, reloaded
we walk towards the crowds that escalate.

I gasp through tear gas and reach the gate
where soldiers strike at shields with wood batons
we chant Peace Peace with crowds that escalate
the bravest rush to film us with their phones.

Soldiers strike their rattan shields with batons
bottles fly as they force an angry path
beat boys with cameras and cell phones
their resistance provokes the soldiers' wrath.

We step across the shards of broken glass
approach the rifles' rage with bleeding feet
the surge of monks provokes the junta's wrath
our tide of crimson robes flows down the street.

I fall beneath the crush of boots and pray
remember me, the monk in Mandalay.

# A Strange Pain

## Quarry III

I sit by the water's edge
dangle my feet
over the reflected dusky sky
and trees growing upside down.
"Careful, it's icy and deep,"
impatience licks his voice,
he's seen me slide the camera from my pocket
and this was supposed to be quick.

It takes time
I want to tell him
to chisel memory,
shape an image or a word
with the bevel of a blade
for posterity. My eye must taste
the woodsy grace
before the lens can see.

He paces on the ledge
close enough
to grab me by the collar
as if he senses I'm thinking of Virginia Woolf,
how easy it would be to stuff
those rocks into my socks and jump,
just jump.
*This is the place*, I murmur,
*where people lose their marbles.*

## Predeceased

You climb the escarpment
once baptized *Mont Royal*
now stripped of trees
and scarred by random piles of rubble
rivulets of molten ash
where pathways lay.

You're old enough
to recollect streams
of hikers, skiers, cyclists
with jackets bright as neon sky.
How long has it been
since sunlight, since snow?

You stumble to the summit
sit with time and pain
to reflect that you're the last to know
there was once a cemetery
on the westward mountainside
the headstones pulverized
then the coffins plundered
after seismic heat
gave way to cold
and they ran out of books to burn.

No funerals anymore
nobody, nothing left to bless
not a flower to love on this planet.
Before memory's effaced
that's what you regret most
the unceremonious
waste.

## Vinci da Leonardo to Homage

Time
transcend
sublimely
you, horses, shells,
wings, hand noble your
escapes nothing. Left to
right expounded arguments,
sketches with brim manuscripts your.
Dragonflies, robots, ears, embryos.
Grace precise with endowed mechanism
as man mortal explore to impelled,
rebuttals with notebooks fill and
antagonists rebuke you
son illegitimate.
Gaze immortal her
mystifies and
drawings your
transcends
time.

## Snarl

The power's out in the night black studio
so we stumble to the shuttered window
grope for the pulley on the wall.
I fumble with the cord
frayed and resistant from disuse.
He takes it, jerks with violence
until the clattering shutters rise.
The light is shrill.
We blink into back alley
Buenos Aires,
the hollow column
between high rises
that shriek in gradient shades
of concrete, glass and steel.
And in mid-air
wires converge
from this and all the other windows
into a taut and twisted mass,
the chats, confessions, taunts
of thousands of *porteños*
residing on this block.
"No wonder the junta's wiretaps
went undetected." He turns from
what he sees as third world chaos
dysfunctional and improvised.
Not so to me.
I recognize that tangle from my heart,
the disarray of dislocated conversations,
the dizziness of their residual
reverberations. I overhear the buzz and hiss
the static through some impulse to resist
while he morphs into that gaucho
all swagger to my vertigo.

## Her Human Voice

She soughs scorched heat to your caress of keys,
her sterling eyes emit a haunting hummmmmm,
her body's slender, black and carved to tease
of grenadilla wood, east African.
From scales and arpeggios you segue
to a *lied*, love's lazy legato tones
twisting into tangos as you soft-tongue
her reed. Low register, melodic moans
crescendo from her bell that amplifies
acoustic accents blown in hard-tongue mode.
Staccatos fire, the syncopation flies
you work the embouchure and riffs explode.
One final thrust of pure machismo
the clarinet fades out pianissimo.

## Amor y Muerte

*I die strangely... It is not life that kills me*
*It is not death that kills me, nor is it love;*
*I die of a thought, mute as a wound...*
*Have you never felt such a strange pain.*

Delmira Agustini, "The Ineffable"
translated by Alejandro Cáceres

Their blood commingles on the floor
where she lies cooling, hair undone
blue silk negligee askew
two bullets shot into her skull.
He's reclining on a sofa bed
warm Smith revolver in his hand.
July 6, 1914, police break down the door
hear him murmuring ...Delmira, Delmira,
his last words, her signature on a scene foreknown
*I die strangely... It is not life that kills me.*

Infamy and carnal carnage
have reporters working through the night
to reconstruct a tabloid narrative.
*¡Amor y muerte!* the headline screams,
ideal couple dead in flagrante
the poet murdered at twenty-seven
her ex-husband dead by his own hand.
They should have quoted her prophecy
expressed in lyrics unadorned, direct,
*It is not death that kills me, nor is it love.*

*El Día*'s details and the bloody snapshot
thrill the little country reputed to be dull.
On the avenues of Montevideo, in carriages
and coffee counters, the bourgeoisie
trade innuendo behind gloved hands.
Did you see the photo...her silken *camisón...*
they must have, you know, before...
She'd have smelled hypocrisy in the bewildered hush
predicted in her book of morning songs
*I die of a thought, mute as a wound...*

She also wrote of drinking death with sombre satisfaction
but by her grave, no one invokes her words
and the writers huddled in the cemetery
allege they're mystified by her film noir demise.
Had she not published three books of verse
they would have burned her manuscripts.
Butterfly by day, vampire at night
she went willingly to his rented room
to ask in ink commingling in a blood stain
*Have you never felt such a strange pain?*

## A Dios

Tango in our bedroom
the night you pack to leave
*adiós muchachos...*
as the open suitcase devours
sweaters, socks, sheet music
and your disassembled clarinet
*con toda mi alma mi bendición…*
two daggers in a box.

You cut through Gardel's ardent throb,
"I left you half a *palta*," and in your Salta Spanish
*avocado* sounds so paltry considering the
watery grace of the Mexican *aguacate.*
Should I desire a sacrament
guacamole spread on wafers
once you've flown away
there's no cilantro, no onions left
to cry me as I slice.

Gardel perished in a plane crash in 1935
but to this day in Chacarita Cemetery
someone leaves a cigarette
between the lips of the tenor's sculpted head
above a handmade sign: Carlos Gardel
may be dead but he sings better every day.
Such devotion in this shrine
no malice in the twist of irony
propped against white lilies in a chalice.

The dance of duelling daggers
plays like a kiss gone awry
soft nips then the bite that draws blood.
Two sincere tears
the tango's meant to wound
*a dios* translates to god.
You snap your suitcase shut
*dos lágrimas sinceras...*
Where're you flying this time?
North, you say, Deception Bay.

## Rendition *n.* (often followed by *of)*

1. *an interpretation of a dramatic role, piece of music, etc.*

He walks across a Frankfurt square through moonlight shifting between the trees. He swings his violin case and whistles a low riff between his teeth, his pace as quick as the Bach invention he just played. Three men encircle him. He's shoved into a Ford Fiesta idling on the cobblestones. Someone stabs him with a needle.

2. *a translation*

He wakes up in a prison cell dressed in a zippered orange jumpsuit. Do you know [name]? Kennen Sie [Name]? He studies the movement of the translator's eyebrows for clues. Where were you on September 5th? Wo waren Sie am fünften September? The raised eyebrows tell him he must remember where he was on that day. Rehearsing? Visiting his sister? He answers their questions with shrugs. They are displeased. He hears them say sedition, admission, deposition, precaution. He is accused. No *of* follows.

3. *a visual representation*

A large metal basin is filled to the brim and placed on a low table in front of his chair. They ask the same questions, he gives the same answers. They push his head down. He swallows water and chokes. They pull him out to ask questions. He coughs and shakes his head. The dirty water smells of sewage. Again and again he drowns. Why water? he asks. It leaves no marks, stupid. You speak English, don't you? Liar. The translator is dismissed.

4. *the act or an instance of giving, yielding or surrendering*

They hand him a form to sign. It happens, they say, some of youse have the same names. He places a check mark in the box stating I did not suffer abuse and is rewarded with his black concert suit, shoes and violin. He is blindfolded and led onto a plane. It lands on an airstrip in Poland. He hitchhikes to Warsaw and boards a train. His eyes ooze pus, his eardrums throb. The violin case rattles on his knees.

## Three Canvas Train Ride

### Wildcat Hills

With the tender shoots of May
the voyage begins in greens
and pointillist yellows that
cheer the gradient hues
brushed into forests, fields and ravines.

I float on the upholstered seat
feet dangle from legs too young to connect
and watch wildcat hills roll by,
repetitive as elementary school
redeemed by glimpses of magic worlds
where princes pose as frogs.

Adults read to me in German
sounds integral as rattling wheels and gears.
I listen to 45s on a portable record player,
fairy tales narrated by famous actors.
*Es war einmal* polished voices intone
and during the dramatic pause
I become *Dornröschen,* Sleeping Beauty.

I whisper to my reflection
while the train whistles
through nighttime towns and pastures.
Daylight breaks and I create
pastoral scenes with wobbling crayons
not yet obsessing over a memorable phrase.

*Grüner als zum Beispiel Rot*
wrote Günter Grass in his poem, "Vermont."
*Greener than for example red*
to my child's eye still cradled in the train
rocking over tracks          unaware of dangers up ahead.

# High Summer

This canvas is a high-speed landscape
with streaks of fiery red encroaching
on August's scorched greens
punctuated by blue and
fuchsia polygons.
My feet feel each vibration
and I'm aware of fluid subtleties
in the light's refraction
as my reflection overlays the frantic foliage.

I'm astonished how much I dwell in my head.
Should I blame those 45s
the fairy tales
my childish whispering?
German is rarely spoken to me now
yet it bridges gaps in my thoughts,
the ensuing silence of the departed.

I have a ritual to ward off pretence,
a counterpoint to hyper-imagination:
on my lap lies a black and white packet,
*Todesanzeigen,* obituaries and *nécrologes*
bound by a red ribbon
that I must retie with a bow
before the ashes of another corpse are strewn.

The train barrels on
through an internal panorama
that's mostly wild, subtropical.
But in lucid intervals
my adult eye can see
the terrifying skyline        amplified.

## *Étapes (décembre)*

The canvas enlarges
to a metropolis of snowed-in
tracks and frosted windows.
Green and red evaporate
into deceivingly static strokes of white
until I perceive the underlying frolic
drifts sculpted by an icy wind
within a slight but emphatic black border.

I've seen others disembark
as pearly flakes drop a curtain
on the night. The train slows,
they are sucked out or fling themselves
onto the track.

I wish to vacate quietly,
to be caught by mosquito netting
and folded into a gentle shroud.
Colours will fade as delicately
as the shimmer of a dragonfly
flitting about until it rests.
Wings folded, it rests.

But this is a blizzard
and I cannot find the memorable phrase
to juxtapose words on a December canvas
with a narrow black frame and I am lost,
frantic. This voyage begun so well in May
should not end this way, absurd
to lose track on a train, the passing
landscapes repeating        the same blank page.

## Dance

She rocks against the harness
in her chair parked by the elevator
her braid's volcanic ash fading down to gold
her face a granite mask
she's slippered but not old
claps her hands three times
and says *j'suis heureuse.*
I pretend her inexistence
as I wait to be delivered from dementia hell
and resort to counting random objects
as if to validate my own lucidity:
six ridges in the scrubbed linoleum
nine lunch trays slotted in a metal rack on wheels
clap clap clap *j'suis heureuse.*
Is she damned to do this in her sleep
or can she sink into a polished, rockless peace?
Clap clap clap *j'suis heureuse*
twelve times a minute outside the nurse's station
where they keep an eye on her while tuning out her mantra.
One time the elevator's stalled
at another floor for the forlorn
she claps *j'suis heureuse* I say *bonjour Madame.*
A nurse explains, "her name's Thérèse
she used to waitress at Ti-Polo
taught line-dancing to seniors in the park at night."
I say *bonjour Thérèse* next time I'm waiting to flee
(just another building in St. Henri, you'd never know)
clap clap clap *j'suis heureuse*
and she thrusts a crumpled page at me
her eyes beseech, I notice now how blue
as I stoop to take her offering.
*Nat & Ses Via-Gras en spectacle chez Ti-Polo*
a flyer dated eighteen months ago
the fissure, pre and post, that separates
the damming of cerebral flow
clap clap clap *j'suis heureuse*
the blinking blues regard me and I sense
she's laughing hard inside.

## A Pacific Vision

The biggest waves wet centre stage
while little ones lap like baby tongues
tasting the splintered edges.

Two musicians play their instruments,
the pianist on the baby grand and
the cellist seated stage left.

This is, it seems, the maddest of visions:
Beethoven's Sonata number 5 in D
filmed on a stage

undulating on open seas
beneath the dazzling skies.
The set defies infinity.

A queasy splash then the cellist introduces
allegro fugato, a lyrical hand extended
but the piano intercedes, the gauntlet to a brawl.

An unhinged quiet, the sun squats
on the horizon and the contest accelerates,
intermittently manic with unsustainable speeds.

The shouting match hurls across the water
a roused chorus of all negated voices
vibrating to a final howl

as piano and cello
unite
in two-note declarations.

Yes no.
Live die.
I am.

The credits roll
and now it's clear
the madman's lucid after all —

chained to the underbelly of the stage
an iron claw lies on the seabed —
his pacific vision is anchored in the deep.

# Pale Blue Light

# Quarry IV

Marble is cold, hard and durable.
It cannot absorb his laughter or its cause.
My lapse is over, I am back
here on this ledge. My feet dangle
above the pond.

Marble's also limestone
in a metamorphic crystalline state,
its wounds will heal eventually
and its scars endure but fade.
He stops pacing
lays his hand on my head
a gentle, warming yet unshakeable restraint.

On the water's stillness
the tarnish of yellow leaves
flecks the looking glass
and the sun's last rays
portray the sculpture of
our bodies thus connected.

This fall of 2005,
I sense the object of my chase
that grain of truth, my quarry.
Existence is confirmed
by the presence of the other,
an echo sounding, *I'm alive.*
This place reminds that chiselling love,
while slow and hard, is still a possibility.

## Cordillera Midnight

In the unseeing
stillness of your vertigo
a *quena* quivers.
The southern constellation
flickers hope from star to star.

## The Last Grenade

one
stone
the dagger
lance and sword
the bayonet and musket
shrapnel, shotguns, shells
the whip and hangman's rope
molotov cocktails and revolvers
the pistol, semi-automatic, drone
B-52s, AK-47s, F-16s, RPMs and WMDs
short-range launchers, fully loaded Humvees
mushroom clouds, neutrons and atom bombs
Katyusha rockets, Kornet and Zelzal missiles
canisters of agent orange, mustard gas
hydrogen, plutonium, uranium, helium
land mines and hand grenades
gas chambers, firing squads
barbed wire, cattle prods
electrocution
guillotines
poison
IED's
...
..
.
lob this discourse of the vicious
let it self-destruct
reuse the fuse
to light a way
with beacons
buoyed by
gentler
words.

## Polar Spheres

You must come on foot
to cross sainted streets in snow-crunching steps.
It must be night, the moon low-rising in the frigid air
a celestial snowball so bright
you will see your shadow's heft
shifting alone across the snow.
Eyes blurred
cheeks chafed
by the condensation of your breath
on wool that mummifies your face
you will shiver
bereft of faith
in this planet poised to implode.
Why not lie down on the frozen rectangle
why not die right here?
From the depth of hopelessness
you will see the distant spheres
lit interiorly as you once were
in rainbow hues
no jagged edge to harm
perched as if just landed on the snow.
Gods and goddesses
descended for a vigil
to remind you
this is beauty                    it still exists
a pre-death spectacle of aching solidarity.
One by one as you approach
to see the giants close      to touch
Venus Saturn Mercury and Mars
their sensors light up shadow shows
within the bubbles' incandescent
glows.                You crunch a dance
just you              the spheres
        atop the earthly snow.

## Nightfall in Sai Gon

usually creeps in unnoticed
through the distracting din of bikes
and hawkers hustling the streets
in counter-torrents of confusion
but that night on the terrace
we witnessed its advance
atop a narrow house
and grasped the seconds
with our eyes like fists held tight
on a brilliant sky deepening
from the hot haze of aqua
into turquoise, sapphire
then the indigo of night

a row of white shirts
pinned by the cuffs of their sleeves
outstretched arms in helpless pleas
hung from a line on the balcony
a pebble's toss across the street
so too our disagreements
held their breath
suspended in the heat
a collective albatross
that lifted with encroaching dusk

this was a lovingly improvised set
four of us seated shoulder to shoulder
before a shaky metal table
spread with a red and yellow beach towel
Australian merlot cooling in a bucket
our glasses resting by plates of
dumplings, rolls and crab claws
sautéed in the first-floor kitchen
sweat raining onto each trayload
ferried up four flights of stairs

to the concrete terrace empty
but for a rusted can of insect repellent
and an electric fan that whirred
whiffs of fish sauce, ginger, garlic into our conversation

of all our nights in Viet Nam
this one remains untarnished
in my memory's film
unlike the grainy scene
on the South China Sea
a week earlier when we'd watched
night invade the bay's empty stretch of sand
in a gust of blackness
leaving only agitated lights
of fishing boats bobbing on invisible waves
recalling images on black-and-white TV
that frantic exodus
on the flimsiest of vessels
and in the thunder we heard history

picture me on a sandy knoll
trying to film a speckled lizard
darting in brittle blades of grass
red spots trembling
against its reptile camouflage
until it found the tunnel home
and pelting rain obscured
the video cam's remaining bytes of memory

*voice-over on the soundtrack*
*14 million tons of bombs & shells dropped*
*70 million litres of toxic chemicals deployed*
*2 million hectares of land destroyed*
*3 million Vietnamese killed from the*
*Da Nang landing of Marines in '65*
*to the withdrawal from Sai Gon in April '75*

but that night
on a terrace in the city
renamed for Ho Chi Minh
the moon ascended
into its patient glow
we trapped the present
sipping chilled
Australian merlot

to the din of motorcycles
taxis, hawkers in the streets below
that vibrated with bustling life
not the rumble of advancing tanks or
the whir of choppers' giant blades
deserting multitudes of outstretched arms

we dipped crab claws and spring rolls
into fish sauce spiked
with potent chilli peppers
that nipped our lips
each bite, each byte
peace, companionship
until the roosters crowed
and Sai Gon's sky
was once again
awash
in pale blue light

## Dac Drums the Drums

Dac drums the drums as if striking at fate
sings old rock & roll while his drumsticks fly.
Chronically almost famous, loved too late
he traps the spotlight with his cymbal's sigh.

He sings sixties' Stones while his drumsticks fly
like he did back in Nam with his brother.
In the army base spotlights, his cymbals would sigh
for the bombing of Hué, his dead father.

An imp with big dreams raised by his brother
he escaped from Saigon, the communist tanks
that entrapped his uniformed stepfather.
No room on the boat for manners or ranks.

Escape from Saigon downplayed as a prank
Dac sewed socks in a Montréal sweatshop,
used manners as a substitute for rank
and books to fuel his swagger to the top.

He moved on from the gig in the sweatshop
bought a new tie, married and had a son
who spurred him to ride for the top
and played guitar to the beat of Dac's drum.

Remarrying, he sang *here comes the sun*
played percussion in a band just for fun,
living his song to the beat of his drum,
the corporate cowboy finally won.

He still plays percussion, learns piano for fun
and calls me in the mornings from his car.
The cowboy nods to his past on the run,
*Cora, can you believe I've come this far?*

Chronically almost famous, loved too late
Dac drums the drums as if striking his fate.

## Warrior

In the gardens by the Emperor's tomb
a man with a weapon on his shoulder
creeps down the embankment and glides into the lake.

He wades past lotus flowers to stand waist-deep,
a shadow poised to pounce
in the shade of frangipani trees.

The scent of almonds hangs humid on the lake
as blossoms sigh and goldfish tease.
The warrior lifts the glinting spear
the tendons on his neck are flexed,
eyes seeking his potential prey
the carp, fat frogs ribbiting in Vietnamese.

For hours he spears the water
each time his harvest fails.
The gong reverberates from a hill above the trees
and he rests his spear against his shoulder
retreats up the embankment

to sit among the monks around a table.
His posture tells the honour of his heritage
persistence, not defeat.

## Itinerant & Stalker

Frozen as the forgotten nickel in your pocket,
you navigate the mottled moonscapes of Sudbury
through dreamlike sulphuric vapours
while I pour oatmeal into stainless steel
my spoon clanging a drone of absence.

In Bathurst you witness the excavation of zinc
conveyed and crushed in subterranean tunnels
as convoluted and as linked as our elemental selves.
I will the sea winds to transmit a message
that claws you home: Bring back fresh lobster!

When you stop for fried catfish at the Throwed Roll Diner
near New Madrid, Missouri and the buxom server
winds up to pitch your roll I muster my mettle,
that ball of aluminum foil rattling 'round my soul,
to thump you into thinking hard of me.

Do you thirst in the Atacama desert,
do the fires of Chuquicamata
smelt your love like copper concentrate,
does your longing for me outweigh the tons of rubble
extracted from the open pit each day?

You stop in Salta to reclaim the version of yourself
carved into the burnished cordillera,
sip maté through a silver straw,
eat empanadas stuffed with pampa beef
while your hot sauce salsas alone.

Long interludes in airport lounges,
global clones of chrome and polyester broadloom.
I say splurge on a Caesar! Raise your glass
into recycled air and toast androgynous automatons
announcing the delays and worse, the bloody cancellations.

In Kristiansand they ply you with aquavit and gravlax,
trade cragged North Sea vistas and fir-lined lakes
for your ironclad expertise. I have no fairy tale name to offer
but can invoke my roots: Estonians are better looking
and much more musical.

Midnight in Ljubljana you linger by the bronze statue of a poet
and drunk on red champagne you confide to him,
"She too writes verse," in slurred Slovenian
and I behold a maudlin sheen
of tears is soldered on your Slavic cheekbones.

Itinerant, I stalk you across continents
and even underground until, cold from altitudes soared,
you taxi on the tarmac home to our stoked
heat in Montréal where the ingot glitters gold
and liquefies.

## Buried Alive

His rebirth is dangerous.
Deep in the Atacama
          copper mine
Omar perspires and prays.
His family holds vigils
in Campamento Esperanza
while three teams
          drill down
          a deep
          dark hole.
The media are thrilled to cover
Operación San Lorenzo
and the patron saint of miners
delivers on day 69.
          Omar Reygadas
          ascends
          in rescue capsule
          Fénix 2.
Wearing Oakley Radar sunglasses
rescued miner 17
steps into his son's embrace
baptized again into Chilean light.
He blesses his newborn grandchild,
submits to dental work and
is interviewed by BBC.
I'm a changed man, Omar says,
born again but I'll go back
into the mine,
          I am a mole.

## Miscarriage

What of the other Omar?
Our Omar, we could say,
lost an eye in battle
was captured at age 15
and is trapped behind the wire.
To protect his shrapnel-damaged
other eye from the glare of Cuban sun
Ottawa sends sunglasses
for this Canadian son not worth a rescue.
What if his name were Stephen?

Omar means "eloquent"
and "long-lived" which means
he'll speak one day
maybe sign a book deal.
But why if not forgiven
would he forgive?
An eye for an eye,
Omar Khadr.

## Small Reveals

For now
because you asked
some small reveals.
I let the door inch open
to a candlelit salon:
a woman with flapper hair
plays harpsichord.
See her iridescent
string of pearls?
A second's glimpse
before I shut that door.
*Aren't those the same pearls*
*you wear sometimes?*
Well, yes, but consider their journey:
saltwater pearls hunted in Asia
strung and purchased in Paris
in the twenties, offered in Estonia
before the divorce,
hidden during the war
through Poland, Germany and Sweden,
worn in the fifties to parties on the Copacabana,
polished for weddings and funerals
in Montevideo, Ottawa and Montréal.
*How did you get the necklace?*
I never met my maternal grandmother
but she lights my heart with her pearls.
*And on the paternal side?*
I'll lift the curtain, let you peek
into the refugee kitchen:
a young woman
yelling in Russian
chases a man
with a knife in her hand.
Of course they divorced,
they were cousins
my grandparents.
That's enough
for now.

## Miraculous Montage of the Morning Mind

let me tell you what I love most
about being alive
(no, it's not you)
it's pressing snooze at six-o-five
when the music plays and thrashing
into stolen slumber, I reconfigure
skunky morning smells
blissful as a kleptomaniac

how shallow
as in lacking depth of knowledge or thought
like a skunk waddling into focus
beneath elm trees at dawn
an urban refugee displaced
family dead or elsewhere
she feasts on the discarded crumbs
of someone's grainy muffin
scavenging things as they come
improvised and self-sufficient

the simulation of filmy frames
transformed by
silver nitrate where black's the
putrescent banana
white's the curving onion peel
and morality's in the garbage can anyway
while sin's in tipping it over
to forage with greedy paws
your trashy is her treasure

viewed through a voyeur's mirror
in a rapid sequence of juxtaposing reflections
which requires me to race
with shallow breath
capture all those images
like a scene shot by Eisenstein
trickster lens panning
to and from the cherubs and the lions

except I focus on
the swizzling sprinkler
silvering striated leaves
on long earthbound boughs
the skunk's enlightened waddle
down the swank of an elmed street

and what I love second most
(still not you)
is the velocity of mind
distance divided by time
equalling the flash with which
the skunk's displaced
by me making love
in the shallows of a lake
with you (finally)
so alive to the contrast
heat in the wetness of cold
the dawn's glow
slicing through elms

this miraculous montage
infinitely flashy
agile and
beyond rank
(like you)
captures the kaleidoscopes
of our splashy rainbow arc
the yin yang
of our arching backs
and serenades
our wake-up song

## Reprise

Remember I once chiselled a quartet
on your abandoned geometry?

Back when autumn's shedding birch trees
flecked the icy stillness of your water.

This summer's thrilling scene
demands a recreation.

Rainbow quilts of towels
drape your graveyard greys.

Delighted screams and yelping dogs
displace the death knell that tolled.

Absurd to think of stuffing socks
and drowning in your pond.

Sunscreen films the water now
beetles picnic on discarded crusts

paws and flip-flopped feet collide
on the slippery marble rocks.

The introspection of that fall
is jostled from your highest ledge

where clusters of bravado
line up to leap.

Kids, sunburned or bronzed,
bicycle the air

plunge into
your crystal depths

and spray their awestruck audience
with cooling shrapnel on this humid August day.

Shrieks of daring, side-stepped mishaps,
the groping, misbegotten kisses all on your watch

in this glorious cove of your embrace
carved into the ever-greening mountainside.

## End Notes

"Before Leaving Hué" was first published in *Descant* (Issue 141, summer 2008) and appeared in *The Best Canadian Poetry in English 2009* (Tightrope Books).

"The Swamp in San Lorenzo" refers to the epic poem, "Martín Fierro," by the Argentine poet José Hernández (1834-1886). The *hornero*, or ovenbird, is Argentina's national bird, known for building oval nests of mud in trees and on telephone poles or fence posts.

"Manifesto of a Murdered Poet" and "Amor y Muerte" are glosas after poems by Delmira Agustini, the Uruguayan poet (1886-1914) killed by her ex-husband in a murder-suicide. The lines cited are from *Selected Poetry of Delmira Agustini – Poetics of Eros*, edited and translated by Alejandro Cáceres (Southern Illinois University Press/Carbondale, 2003).

"Response" refers to the poem by W.H. Auden, "Friday's Child," which he wrote in memory of Dietrich Bonhoeffer, the pastor and writer imprisoned by the Nazis and executed shortly before the end of World War II.

"The Quena Testifies," set in Machu Picchu, refers to the Andean instrument dating back to the time of the Incas. The *quena* is a single flute made of cane or bamboo.

"Vinci da Leonardo to Homage" pays tribute to the artist's timelessness and curiosity. The form, a double ethere, is best read from bottom to top and right to left.

"Her Human Voice" appeared in the *Literary Review of Canada* (Vol. 21, No. 1, January/February 2013).

In "Three Canvas Train Ride," the subtitles *Wildcat Hills*, *High Summer* and *Étapes (décembre)* refer to paintings in the Montréal Museum of Fine Arts by, respectively, Ivan Eyre, Hans Hofmann and Charles Gagnon.

"Polar Spheres" is a response to *Sphères polaires*, an installation created by Bernard Duguay and Pierre Gagnon, Lucion Média in the Quartier des spectacles, Montréal, December 2010.

## Acknowledgements

My profound admiration and thanks go to poet George Payerle for his cantankerous buckaroo mind and brilliance in editing this collection. Heartfelt thanks also go to Karen Haughian and her team at Signature Editions for their efforts and support.

I am grateful to the poets and writers who have enriched my thinking with their immense creativity, especially Marie-Elisabeth Morf, Alexina Scott-Savage and Lady Rojas Benavente. Thanks also to Michael Helm and the Humber School for Writers as well as the Banff Centre.

To my brother Hendrik, thank you for teaching me the word *conscience* when I was three and for all the subsequent years of your intellectual insights.

This collection is dedicated to Otokar with our motto: *amor & cachondeo.*

## About the Author

Cora Siré writes poetry, essays and fiction. Her poems have appeared in *Descant,* the *Literary Review of Canada, The Best Canadian Poetry in English 2009* (Tightrope Books) and *Sus huellas son letras* (Éditions Alondras, 2011). Born in Canada, she often writes of elsewheres, both real and imaginary, drawing on her encounters in realms ranging from Argentina to Vietnam and her family's history of displacement. She lives in Montréal.

ECO-AUDIT
*Printing this book using Rolland Opaque 50 instead of virgin fibres paper saved the following resources:*

| Trees | Solid Waste | Water | Air Emissions |
| --- | --- | --- | --- |
| 1 | 18kg | 1,462 L | 164 kg |